Coins

From human remains (usually bones) archaeologists can find out how tall and how healthy people were, learning even more about how well they ate and what kind of lives they led.

Treasure-hunters or historians?

Early archaeologists were interested in finding beautiful or expensive objects!

Later archaeologists are a bit like historians and a bit like scientists. They are interested in discovering and recording the past, but instead of books they use tools and equipment and follow strict methods.

Archaeologists carefully excavate a site

One of the first people to act like this was an Englishman, William Pitt Rivers (1827–1900). He is called 'The Father of Scientific Archaeology' because he collected and catalogued (recorded) all the artefacts he dug up, not just the beautiful ones, and he saw the importance of studying everyday objects to understand the past.

Planning an excavation

When archaeologists excavate a site, they first mark out the area into squares using flags, stakes and string. This is so they can record exactly where everything is found. They dig very carefully using trowels and hoes, and draw plans and take photographs to record what they find. Tools like spoons, dental picks and small brushes are used to make sure nothing is damaged as it is dug from the ground. However, the most important tools an archaeologist uses are their notebook and pencil to write down what they find!

Radio carbon dating

In 1960, an American scientist called Willard F. Libby won the Nobel Prize for Chemistry for inventing a process called 'Radio carbon dating'. Radio carbon dating measures how much 'carbon-14' (a radioactive version of carbon) there is in plant or animal remains – the older something is, the less carbon-14 there will be because it will have decayed to a non-radioactive state. By measuring the age of remains discovered on a site, archaeologists can work out when the site was inhabited. This is very useful, especially as many people throughout history have lived in the same places and the artefacts they leave behind can sometimes get muddled up!

Aerial survey

Modern archaeologists can use technology to help them in their work. An example of this is an aerial survey, when pictures of an area are taken from high above it (from a plane or helicopter). Remains under the ground can cause changes above the ground. For example, plants growing above a buried wall may grow more slowly than usual. These differences can be seen from above. An aerial survey can help archaeologists plan where to dig or to see the layout of entire houses or cities.

Why do archaeologists use metal detectors?

These can find things like old jewellery and belt-buckles, and can be used to find cannonballs on an old battlefield.

What do we sometimes call an excavation?

A dig.

The Aztecs

The Aztecs were the last native American rulers of Mexico. Around the end of the 12th century, their wandering tribe left its home in the north and settled in the Valley of Mexico, which they called 'Anahuac'. Here they built their capital city, Tenochtítlan. Over the next 200 years, the Aztecs built a powerful empire of around 12 million people.

Tenochtítlan

In Tenochtítlan the Aztecs built awe-inspiring temples and giant pyramids where they sacrificed captured prisoners to their gods by cutting out their hearts. They had a mighty army and grew rich by collecting tributes (payments) from all the tribes they conquered.

Aztec jade mask

The Aztec gods

As farmers, the Aztecs depended heavily on the forces of nature and worshipped many of them as gods. Their chief god was Huitzilopochtli, the sun god and god of war. Other gods worshipped were Tlaloc (the god of rain), Quetzalcoatl the Feathered Serpent (the god of wind and learning), and Tezcatlipoca the Smoking Mirror (god of the night sky). The Aztecs believed they had to keep their 'good' gods strong by making human sacrifices to them – if they failed to do this, they believed other 'evil' gods would destroy the world. The Aztec priests used stone-bladed knives to cut out the hearts of up to 1,000 people a week and offer them to the sun god. Most of the people sacrificed were captured war prisoners, though Aztec warriors would sometimes volunteer for the most important rituals – they believed it was a great honour to be chosen. According to legend, in 1487 Aztec priests sacrificed more than 80,000 prisoners of war at the dedication of the rebuilt temple of the sun god!

The Aztecs built elaborate water systems for their cities

The fall of the Aztec Empire

The great Aztec Empire came to an end suddenly. In 1519, when Aztec civilisation was at its height, Spanish explorers ('conquistadors') arrived in Mexico led by a man named Hernán Cortés. The Spanish made war on the Aztecs and defeated them. The last independent Aztec Emperor, Montezuma II, was captured by the Spanish and killed. The Aztec Empire crumbled and the Spanish invaders took over.

Art and writing
The Aztecs wrote in small pictures called 'pictographs'. This form of writing was very difficult to learn and was mainly done by priests or scribes.

The Aztecs made wonderful jewellery using gold, silver, copper, emerald, turquoise and jade (they prized jade above all other materials). They also fashioned vividly-dyed cloth, dramatic stone sculptures and elaborate garments made of the feathers of tropical birds.

The story of Tenochtitlán

At first, the Aztecs were a poor, ragged people, driven from place to place. Then their leader, Tenoch, had a vision. The sun god Huitzilopochtli told him to lead his people to a swampy island in the middle of Lake Texcoco. There he should look for an eagle perched on a cactus, eating a serpent. On that spot, they were to build their city. The city they built in about 1325 was named Tenochtitlán ('the city of Tenoch') and was built on one natural and several artificial islands in the swampy lake. The Aztecs built bridges and causeways to connect the city to the mainland, and canals to enable people to move around easily. The city quickly grew from a collection of mud huts and small temples to the capital city of a mighty empire – by 1519 about 60,000 people lived or did business there. Today Mexico City stands in the same place.

Stone knife, used for human sacrifices

Two calendars

The Aztecs had two calendars, a religious one and a solar one. The religious calendar told them when to consult their gods. The solar calendar was used to fix the best time for planting crops. A religious year had 260 days. A solar year had 365 days – 18 months of 20 days each and 5 'spare' days.

Q&A?

Did the Aztecs play musical instruments?

Yes, especially during religious ceremonies. The most common instruments were rattles, whistles, trumpets, flutes, copper bells, and shells.

What did the Aztecs eat?

Corn was their main crop. Women ground the corn into coarse flour to make flat corn cakes called tortillas, which were their principal food. Other crops included beans, chilli peppers, squash, avocadoes and tomatoes.

Stone solar calendar

Castles

When we use the word 'castle', we most often mean a self-contained fortress built to defend against enemies and control the area around it. Besides being used for protection, castles sometimes served as residences for the lord or monarch. During the Middle Ages, feudal lords who wanted to protect their people and expand their power built large numbers of castles all over Europe.

Early castles

The first castles were constructed of wood and so were easily destroyed by fire. Later castles were built of stone and were therefore much more robust. Many early stone castles consisted of a single tower. As time went on, however, castles became bigger, more elaborate and better designed for defence. Many of these castles survive today.

Where were castles built?

When possible, castles were built in places that were easy to defend, such as hills, mountain passes, peninsulas, and islands in lakes. They were often built to protect important strategic places such as ports and river crossings. For example, Stirling Castle in Scotland is built at a cross of the River Forth.

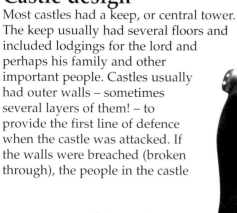

Castel Nuovo, Naples, Italy

Castle design

Most castles had a keep, or central tower. The keep usually had several floors and included lodgings for the lord and perhaps his family and other important people. Castles usually had outer walls – sometimes several layers of them! – to provide the first line of defence when the castle was attacked. If the walls were breached (broken through), the people in the castle

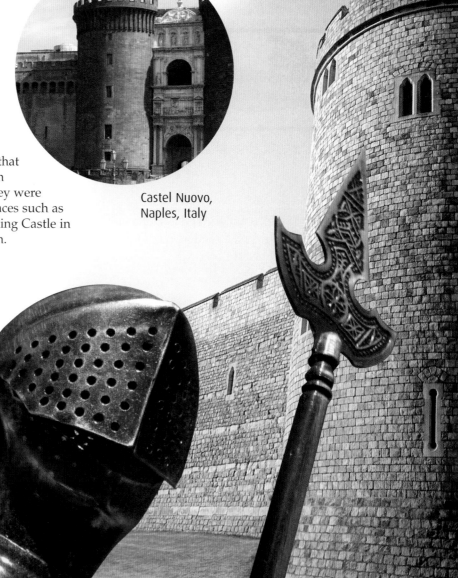

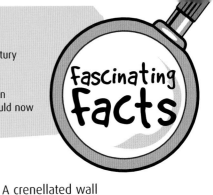
Many English castles were destroyed or badly damaged during the Civil War of the 17th century because Oliver Cromwell wanted to remove all traces of royal power.

The word dungeon comes from the French word *donjon*, meaning tower or keep. Prisoners in medieval castles were more often held in the highest room of a tower than in what we would now call a 'dungeon'.

could retreat into the keep. When many people needed protection, walls could be built around a whole city or town (for example, Carcassonne in France). In addition to the outer walls, castles had towers and battlements from which to watch for enemies. Castles with round towers were more difficult to attack because rocks bounced off the curved walls.

A crenellated wall

Defending a castle

Inside the castle defenders would have a good view of their attackers from the high battlements and towers and would use bows and arrows to keep them away. There were often small slits so that archers could fire their arrows without being hit themselves. If attackers got close to the castle and put tall ladders up the walls, those inside would pour boiling water and hot sand onto them from the tops of the walls to keep them away. After the invention of gunpowder in the 13th century, however, defending a castle became harder and harder.

Castles under siege

When the castle was under attack it was said to be 'under siege'. Attackers would try many different ways to take over the castle. They would climb the walls or break them down by throwing heavy rocks at them, using machines such as catapults. Battering rams would be used to try to break down the gates. If a siege went on for a long time the attackers might try to starve out those who lived there by ensuring that no new supplies could get in.

Castles since the Middle Ages

By the late 1600s, gunpowder and artillery had become so effective that castles were no longer useful for defence. As life became more peaceful, many of the castles that still survived were used for other purposes. For example, in the Scottish highlands, castles were often used as courts to settle disputes that were presided over by the laird. Others, such as the Tower of London and the Bastille in Paris, were used as prisons. Today many castles survive as monuments to the past, and large numbers of people visit them every year.

Q&A?

What is the 'iron ring' of castles?

This is a series of strong stone castles built in Wales by King Edward I (1239–1307) to control the Welsh population. They include the castles of Caernarfon, Harlech and Conwy.

Where does the word 'castle' come from?

It comes from the Latin word castellum, *meaning fortress. The word* castrum, *used for the wooden forts built by Roman soldiers, means a fortified place.*

7

Explorers

Human beings have always been explorers. Ever since cavemen set out to discover what lay beyond the horizon, we have been fascinated by the unknown and the undiscovered.

The promise of adventure

Nowadays we have complicated and detailed maps of the world. We learn all about geography and the peoples of other lands in school, and we can go to zoos or read in books about animals like lions and elephants. But imagine setting sail across an ocean not knowing what you would find, or being the first person from your country ever to see an elephant! Exciting adventures like these, and the promise of great treasure, have led people to become explorers, despite knowing they would face terrible dangers.

Early European explorers

As people learned to read and write they began to leave records of their travels. The medieval explorer Marco Polo (1254–1324) was the first person to cross the whole of Asia and to leave journals of what he had seen. Many great European explorers followed his example, returning from their travels with new maps and new treasures, and astonishing tales of the strange animals and plants and ways of life they had discovered.

The age of discovery

The 15th and 16th centuries are known as the 'age of discovery'. At that time rival European countries, hungry for treasure and power, had powerful ships and navigational tools to help them sail the oceans in search of new lands. The Spanish king Charles I gave the Portuguese sailor Ferdinand Magellan (1480–1521) five ships, and he set sail in 1519 on the first circumnavigation of (journey around) the globe. Many of his crew survived and the expedition was a success, but Magellan himself died during the voyage. The second successful circumnavigation was made by an English privateer called Francis Drake (1542–1596). Drake was supported by Queen Elizabeth, who provided him with ships and supplies in return for a large share of the treasures he promised to find. Although Drake sailed around the world, the treasures with which he presented Elizabeth were actually stolen from Spanish galleons!

Treasures from the East

Many explorers did return with treasures, although not the gold and silver they dreamed of finding, but instead things like silks and spices from the Orient (right). Spices were at one time thought even more valuable than gold. They were highly prized by the wealthy for flavouring and preserving their food. For this reason we can see why the Portuguese explorer Vasco da Gama (1460–1524) became famous for discovering a new and fast trading route to India.

New territories

When explorers went looking for gold they found other treasures and sometimes discovered places by accident. This was not surprising, because they didn't have good maps and believed the earth was much smaller than it is. The most famous of all these accidents is the discovery of the Americas by Christopher Columbus. Columbus set sail in 1492 thinking that, because the world was round, sailing west would get him to the rich East more quickly and safely. Not knowing that America existed, he sailed right into it!

Modern explorers

Since the age of discovery, exploration has continued. Explorers have discovered tribes in the heart of African rainforests, reached the North and South Poles and explored deep oceans in submarines. Scientists such as plant hunters often search for undiscovered species that may provide the raw ingredients for new drugs to help cure disease.

Perhaps the most exciting place we have yet to explore fully is the vastness of space, into which we send satellites and probes. One day astronauts may set out to travel to other planets just as Magellan and Columbus travelled to other lands!

Christopher Columbus sailed over 5,000 miles of open seas.

The plant hunters of previous centuries brought us many of the plants we see in our gardens today. For example, tulips originally grew only in Turkey (below).

Q&A?

Why do we sometimes refer to Native Americans as "Indians"?

That is what Christopher Columbus mistakenly called them, thinking he was in the East Indies!

What is Il Milione?

That is the original name of Marco Polo's book about his travels to China. The name comes from Polo's family nickname, Emilione. We usually call the book 'The Travels of Marco Polo'.

Gandhi

Mohandas Karamchand Gandhi was born in Porbandar, Gujarat, India in 1869. He is more commonly known as Mahatma Gandhi ('Mahatma' means 'Great Soul' in Sanskrit), or Bapu, which in many Indian languages means 'father'. He became a great spiritual and political leader, and led the successful campaign for India's independence from Britain. He inspired the civil rights movement in America, and the movement to end racism and division in South Africa.

His family was Hindu, and so from an early age he followed that religion's teachings. These included being vegetarian (not eating meat), not harming living creatures, respecting others, and fasting (not eating or drinking for a long time) to cleanse the body. He did badly at school, and only just got in to Bombay University. He had heard that England was 'the very centre of civilisation', and he came to London in 1888, to study Law. However, he could not stomach the English food, and of course refused to eat meat, so he became a very active vegetarian, joining societies and writing articles about vegetarianism.

South Africa

As a young man, Gandhi was quiet, and not very interested in how the world was run. He often got very nervous in court. He started to change after he went to work in South Africa, in 1893. Several events made him start to stand up for himself and the rights of his countrymen. One of these was when a court judge asked him to remove his turban. Gandhi refused and stormed out of the court. Another time, a train conductor tried to make Gandhi move from First Class to Third, even though he had a First Class ticket. Gandhi used his lawyer's training to sue the company, and he won!

After learning of the racism, oppression and injustices towards Indians in South Africa, he started to become an active protester. He organised petitions to stop the government taking away the Indians' right to vote in elections and he founded the Natal Indian Congress in 1894.

Return to India

After 20 years helping his fellow Indians in South Africa, Gandhi returned to India to help people in his homeland. In the Champaran district, he helped poor farmers to get a better deal, and to raise standards of living in the poor, country villages. Then, in the Punjab, British Indian Army

soldiers massacred 379 Indian men, women and children at Amritsar in 1919. This caused deep anger in India, and there was an increase in protesting, rioting and violence.

But Gandhi did not believe in violence. Gandhi had developed the idea of peaceful non-cooperation in South Africa. It was known as the 'satyagraha', or 'devotion to truth'.

The Indian National Congress, a political party, accepted Gandhi's idea of non-violence, and made him leader of their party. From then on, Gandhi started leading towards independence.

Satyagrahas

By 1920, Gandhi was a leading figure in Indian politics. He organised satyagrahas against the government. They were always peaceful. For example, the Indians would boycott (stop buying) British goods to harm the British economy.

Unfortunately, Gandhi was arrested in 1922, and imprisoned for six years. He was released after only two years, but by this time the Indian National Congress had broken apart. Gandhi did not achieve much for several years, until the Calcutta Congress in 1928, where he demanded full independence from the British for India.

Final message of peace

Gandhi continued to negotiate with the British government for many years, and in 1945 he started negotiations with the new Labour government. In 1947, a plan was formed to create the separate, independent nations of India and Pakistan. India would be a Hindu country, and Pakistan a Muslim country.

The old nation of India was divided, though, and there was rioting. Gandhi appealed for calm, and went on a fast, which stopped the rioting. Sadly, Gandhi was shot dead by a young Hindu fanatic before he could see India become fully independent.

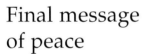

To which Prime Minister of India was Gandhi a mentor?

Jawaharlal Nehru (1889–1964), first Prime Minister of India.

When was the first satyagraha?

This was Gandhi's passive resistance to British rule in India.

Gandhi is remembered as a man of peace and great wisdom. His message of peace and love will live on. As he said himself:

'When I despair, I remember that all through history the way of truth and love has won. There have been tyrants and murderers and for a time they seem invincible, but in the end, they always fall.'

He was assassinated in 1948.

fascinating facts

Gandhi's birthday, October 2nd, is commemorated each year in India as Gandhi Jayanti, and it is a public holiday. There is also a Gandhi series of currency (money) in India.

Gandhi was nominated for the Nobel Peace Prize five times, but did not win it once.

The Greeks

I n the period before the Roman empire, from about 776 BC to the death of Alexander in 323 BC, ancient Greece was the most important civilisation in western Europe. The ancient Greeks lived in a society that valued individual freedom within the law, and promoted excellence in sport, learning and the arts. Greek civilisation has left us many legacies, including many of the words we use today and the Olympic Games.

Ancient Greece was not a single nation, but made up of a number of city-states called polis which were dotted across the mainland, the islands of the Aegean and Ionian seas, and along the coast of what is now Turkey.

Athens, named after Athena, the goddess of wisdom and the city's patron, was the intellectual centre of Greece, and one of the first city-states.

Culture

The artistic talents of the Athenians can be viewed through many different forms which have survived for centuries, such as architectural designs, sculptures, pottery and fine jewellery.

At the Theatre of Dionysia, named after the god of wine, a religious festival was held in honour of the gods. For ten days Athenians filled the theatre to see plays performed by their favourite poets and playwrights. Women were not allowed to take part. The men wore elaborate masks and costumes while performing both male and female roles.

The Olympics

The Olympic Games were the greatest national festival for the Athenians. Held every four years, athletes came from all regions of Greece to compete in the great Stadium of Olympia and honour their supreme god, Zeus. At the conclusion of the games, the winners were presented with garlands and crowned with olive wreaths.

Life in ancient Greece

Athenian soldiers were required to serve two years in the military. After the first year, they were given a sword and a shield with the state's emblem on it. Although they served only two years, they could be called at any moment up to the age of sixty. Most wars between city-states were due to problems concerning harvests or livestock, and lasted only a day or so. Heralds were government officials who travelled throughout Greece carrying important messages for their city-states. They held a special stick as a sign of their authority and were under the protection of the messenger god Hermes – people were not allowed to attack them, even during war, as this was seen as breaking international law. Farmers kept goats, sheep, pigs and chickens. Crops were grains, grapes and olives. Gods were usually served by priests in

Why did the actors play male and female roles?

Women were not allowed to participate in dramatic activities.

What was the most important event at the Olympic Games?

The pentathlon, where an athlete competed in five different events.

ancient Greece, and goddesses were served by priestesses. Often the job was for life, but some priests and priestesses were

ordinary citizens who served for two to four years, or just during religious festivals. Their duties ranged from supervising rituals and taking part in festivals, to conducting weddings and funerals.

Mythology

The Gods were described as having essentially human, but ideal bodies.

Zeus was the chief god. The gods and goddesses were said to live on Mount Olympia. Each god or goddess had a particular area of interest. For example, Poseidon was god of the sea, Persephone goddess of the seasons, Apollo drove his chariot across the sky for the sun. Greek gods were said to have many fantastic abilities, such as being able to disguise themselves, transport themselves to any location, are not affected by disease, can be wounded only under highly unusual circumstances, and they are immortal.

This is a collection of stories that explain how the world began and described the lives of the gods and goddesses as well as of the ordinary people. The stories are passed down to us through oral and written traditions as well as from vase paintings.

The Cyclops were giants who were thrown into the underworld by their brother Cronus. But Zeus, son of Cronus, released the giants and in gratitude they gave him the gifts of thunder and lightning. So he became ruler of the Olympian gods.

Letters from the Greek alphabet are still used today, especially in science. Examples are α, β, γ, μ, θ, π and Ω. For example, the formula for finding the area of a circle $c = \pi \times radius^2$.

Fascinating Facts

Industry and the industrial revolution

Major changes in the way many people lived and worked took place in the late 18th century and early 19th century. This period of history is known as the industrial revolution. At this time there were rapid developments in technology and communication that had a very significant impact on people's lives in many parts of the world, especially in the USA and Europe.

Life before the industrial revolution

Up to the time of the industrial revolution most people lived and worked at home or nearby, mostly in villages or small towns. People worked on the land as farmers, or spun yarn and wove cloth on looms in their homes for making clothes, and sold their produce at markets to make a living and support their families.

Machinery before the industrial revolution

Until the invention of the steam engine most small machinery was driven by water or wind power. Water wheels and windmills

harnessed the power of water and wind to grind wheat into flour. However, the wind and water on which these mills relied could not be depended on to flow at a constant rate.

Technological developments

Steam power

Steam power was first used to pump water from coal mines at the end of the 17th century but it was not until late in the 18th century that James Watt invented an improved and reliable steam engine with a separate condenser chamber. This steam engine, which was powered by burning coal, could be used to drive machinery in a mill or factory.

Where did the American industrial revolution begin?

The American industrial revolution began in Lowell, Massachusetts. Lowell was America's first planned industrial city.

When did coal mining first begin?

Possibly in China in about 50 BC, and certainly the Romans used coal when they were in England. In America the Aztecs were using coal for heating and for making ornaments. By the Medieval period in Britain coal was being extracted from small-scale pits, but it was not until the industrial revolution that the mines employed lots of people.

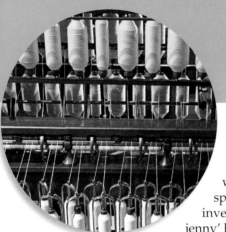

Spinning jenny
Spinning yarn from wool, cotton or flax was speeded up by the invention of the 'spinning jenny' by James Hargreaves in the 18th century. The process was much quicker by machine – previously people had worked on individual spinning wheels.

The first factories

As inventions such as the spinning jenny were developed, some industrialists saw the potential for bringing the different processes needed to make goods together in one place. This is how factories began. Richard Arkwright, an inventor who was also an entrepreneur, built some of the first mill factories to make yarn and weave it into cloth.

The development of towns and cities

As the factory system developed, people moved away from the countryside. Large towns and cities were built to house the workers and the factories. Children would work from a very young age, often in dangerous jobs such as cleaning underneath large machines such as looms. The factories were usually very noisy places where people worked long hours.

Transport

Canals
Alongside the development of industry into large factories methods of transport were developed to transport raw materials in and finished goods out. In the late 18th century canals allowed bulky raw materials, such as china clay, and fragile goods, such as pottery to be transported safely. Horses were used to pull the barges.

Railways
From the middle of the 19th century the development of the steam engine for steam locomotives meant that railway development progressed very rapidly in many parts of the world. Many railways were built close to the canals following the same routes between towns and cities and to and from the coast for speed and efficiency in trading. In addition to the metal tracks, which were required for the trains to run on many bridges across rivers had to be built.

Fascinating Facts

One of the first safety lamps for coal miners, known as the Davy lamp, was named after its inventor Sir Humphrey Davy. Poisonous gases could be ignited by the flames on miners' candles. The safety lamp kept the flame safely within a gauze so that it could not ignite the gases. Before the invention of safety lamps miners carried canaries with them. The canaries were extremely sensitive to the presence of poisonous gas in the mines and would die very quickly, thus alerting the miners to the danger. Despite the use of safety lamps, canaries were still taken into coal mines in Britain until late in the 20th century.

The first cast iron bridge in the world was built across the River Severn at the town which became known as Ironbridge near Shrewsbury, England. This area is often called the birthplace of the industrial revolution, being near to Coalbrookdale where iron was first smelted with coke. Ironbridge became part of a World Heritage Site in 1986.

The Middle Ages

The Middle Ages in Europe are commonly dated from the end of the Roman Empire in the 5th century until the early 16th century. They are often called the medieval period (sometimes spelled 'mediaeval' or 'mediæval').

In Europe during the 12th and 13th centuries, there was a radical change in the rate of new inventions: cannons and spectacles and silk appeared, and compasses were introduced from the east. There were also improvements to ships and clocks which made exploration possible.

The Feudal System

People in the Middle Ages lived under a way of life known as the Feudal System. In this system, the King gave land to his knights and nobles in return for them lending him troops and fighting for him themselves in time of war. The nobles (lords) let peasants live on and farm their land. In return for this, the peasants farmed the land and paid rent to the landlord. This rent was not paid in money but by giving the landlord some of their crops.

Strip farming

Life for ordinary people was very hard. Unlike today, where farmers farm large fields of crops, in the Middle Ages the land was divided into small strips, which each peasant family would farm. Farming methods were very basic, and often the crops would fail, meaning the people would not have enough to eat. The fields were ploughed with a team of oxen pulling a plough. Peasants hoed and harvested their own strips, but worked together on big jobs such as ploughing or haymaking. Working together was essential, as a failed harvest could mean starvation for the whole village. Life for the rich was much more pleasant. They lived in big castles and manor houses. They wore bright clothing made of expensive material, and went hunting. They would have big feasts where there was lots to eat and drink.

Religion

Religion was very important during the Middle Ages. There was one predominant religion in Europe: Catholic Christianity. Church services were conducted in Latin, the scholarly and diplomatic language of the day. The Church controlled most aspects of everyday life. The Church grew very powerful during this time, partly because people would give land and money to the Church when they died. Many churches and cathedrals were built across Europe, such as the Cathedral of St. Michael (right) and St. Gudula in Brussels, Belgium. Also, many people became monks or nuns, and lots of monasteries were built.

The Crusades

Religion was also the reason for one of the longest wars in history, the Crusades. These were a religious war, to try to free Jerusalem and the Holy Land from the Muslims. Rulers went on crusades. Richard I of England (1157–1199) and Philip II of France agreed to go on the Third Crusade together, since each feared that, in his absence, the other would take his territories. When the Christian soldiers returned from the Crusades, they brought back many ideas, goods, and inventions from the Arab world. Westerners adopted the Arabic system of counting, which is the one we still use today. Previously, people had used Roman numerals, which you can sometimes still see today on clock or watch faces. Some clocks were designed showing both systems.

The Black Death

This disease (bubonic plague) killed between a third and two-thirds of Europe's population between 1347 and

1351. It changed Europe's social structure and was a serious blow to the Catholic Church. The uncertainty of survival influenced people to live for the moment.

Gunpowder

Gunpowder was also introduced into Europe during the 14th century as a weapon of war. Before this, the only weapons available were swords, axes, etc. It had been invented in China and used for both weapons and fireworks. At first, early guns were dangerous. In fact, they were more likely to kill the person firing them than the intended target, because they were so unreliable. Later, though, as the guns became more reliable, gunpowder changed warfare greatly.

The written word

The printing press, which was also a Chinese invention, became popular in Europe at the end of the 14th century. It meant that books could be produced more quickly, cheaply, and reliably. People were able to buy books for themselves, meaning that knowledge could spread throughout the world more quickly.

 **Q&A?**

What other inventions were brought to Europe during the Middle Ages?

The abacus (a machine for counting), buttons, and paper money.

Why were church services read in Latin?

Latin was the ancient language of the Roman Empire, where the Christian Church began.

Medieval scientists believed that all things were made up of four basic elements: earth, air, fire, and water. They thought that if they were combined in the right amounts, any substance could be made. They even thought they could turn lead into gold! This science was called Alchemy.

During the Middle Ages, nearly a third of every year was given over to religious holidays.

fascinating facts

Native American peoples

The Native American peoples are the tribes of people who were living in America before Europeans settled there. Christopher Columbus (c. 1451–1506), sailing from Spain, thought he had found a new route to the Indies but found the Americas instead. He did not know America existed, so he called the tribes he met 'Indians'. For a long time they were known as 'American Indians'.

Native American tribes

Native Americans are thought to have migrated (moved to live) from Siberia over 11,000 years ago. They were able to do this because during the Ice Age there was a 'land bridge' joining these two continents. They settled into many largely peaceful tribes all across America, forming small hunting and farming communities. America is a very large country and the land and weather vary considerably. Many hundreds of Native American tribes lived across America, living in ways that suited their territory. Each tribe had different traditions, art and religious beliefs, and also different languages.

North-west

In the north-west it was warm with lots of rain and woodland. The Haida, the Tsimshian and the Nootka lived on a diet of salmon, wild fruits and berries. They lived in wooden houses, sailed wooden canoes, ate from wooden bowls and even wore tightly woven wooden hats to keep out the heavy rains! Some tribes had totem poles, large wooden poles carved with symbolic animals, telling the history and legends of the tribe.

Central plains

On the dry, grassy central plains some Native American tribes were farmers, living in dome-shaped earthen houses and farming corn and beans. Other tribes were nomads, living in movable 'tepees' (houses made from animal skins stretched over a wooden frame) and hunting bison. The huge bison supplied almost everything the nomadic tribes needed to stay alive – meat for food, bone for tools and skins for housing and clothing.

Central plateau

The Spokan, the Paiute and the Shoshone lived in the rocky central plateau area. They gathered food like roots and fruit and also hunted small animals. They made acorn

Which Disney movie is based on the life of a Native American woman?

Pocahontas.

What is a pow-wow?

A Native American get-together, for making tribal decisions or for celebration, often involving ceremonial dancing and drumming.

bread by pounding acorns and mixing them with hot water. They often lived in shelters like the tepees of the plains tribes, but instead of animal skins the pole frame was covered with woven mats of plants and reeds. These were called 'wickiups'.

Eastern woodlands

In the eastern woodlands lived deer-hunters, the Natchez, the Choctaw and the Cherokee. They lived in dome-shaped 'wigwams' or in long wooden houses and wore deerskin clothing. The men were hunters and the women farmed small gardens of corn and beans.

Northern areas

The northern areas were hard places to live. The Chipewyan hunted caribou (native American moose), caught fish and gathered berries and edible roots. They lived in caribou-skin tents, and made nets and bags for hunting and laces for their snowshoes from caribou leather thongs.

South-west

In the south-west the Hopi lived in towns built into cliffs and canyons called 'pueblos'. They were farmers, growing corn and beans. They also grew cotton which they wove into fabric for their own clothes and blankets and to trade with other tribes for things like buffalo meat. The men wove cloth and worked the farms. Women made pottery, decorated in many colours.

The Europeans

The arrival of the Europeans had a huge effect on Native Americans and their way of life. The European presence introduced at least a dozen strange diseases during this era that American Indians had no natural immunity against. It is believed that more native people died due to foreign diseases than were lost in wars fighting for their homelands.

Fascinating Facts

Wampum are strings of knots and beads used by the Iroquois to record tribal tales. They are also used as a unit of measure (for counting).

Some words in English have Native American origins:
- Kayak, from the Yupik word 'quayq'
- Igloo, from the Inuit word 'iglu', meaning 'house'
- Moose, from the Abenaki word 'mos'
- Pecan, from the Illinois word 'pakani'
- Toboggan, from the Micmac word 'topaghan'

The Norman conquest

The Battle of Hastings, in 1066, is one of the most famous battles fought on British soil, and changed English life forever. There were actually two invasions of England in 1066. Without the first one, the Norman conquest might never have succeeded.

In 1066 the Anglo-Saxon King of England, Edward the Confessor, died without leaving any sons to inherit his throne. The kingship was then claimed by three men: Earl Harold Godwinson of Wessex, Duke William of Normandy, and Harald Hardrada, Viking King of Norway.

Earl Harold

Earl Harold was an adviser to Edward the Confessor, and the king's brother-in-law. He claimed that Edward had named him as his heir. The Anglo-Saxon high council, the Witan, preferred Harold to the foreign claimants, and Harold was crowned on the same day Edward was buried.

Duke William of Normandy

William was a distant blood relation of Edward the Confessor. He said Edward had chosen him as his heir a long time before. The Normans insisted Harold had sworn on holy relics to support William's claim to the throne. When Edward died childless and Harold took the English throne for himself, William considered that Harold had broken his promise.

Who were the Anglo-Saxons?

The Anglo-Saxons were the dominant people in England from 410 to 1066.

Who was the last Anglo-Saxon King of England?

King Harold was the last Anglo-Saxon King of England.

Harald Hardrada

Harald became ruler of Norway after his nephew King Magnus died. Magnus had made a pact with King Harthacnut, a previous ruler of England, that if either one of them died childless, then the other would inherit his kingdom. Harald claimed that, as Magnus's heir, he was therefore the rightful King of England.

The battle of Stamford Bridge

Almost as soon as King Harold was crowned, he had to get ready to fight for his new throne: news came that Harald Hardrada had landed with an army in the north of England.

King Harold rushed north with his hastily raised army, and on 25 September defeated the Vikings in a surprise attack at Stamford Bridge. Harald Hardrada was killed, and only 24 ships from his invasion fleet of 300 made it back to Norway.

While King Harold was defeating the Viking threat, Duke William had already started his own invasion. Harold's men were still celebrating their victory in the north when news came that William had invaded in the south, landing on 28 September.

The battle of Hastings

To fight William, King Harold and his men had to march 400 km (250 miles) from Stamford Bridge to Hastings. They did this in just nine days, but they were tired.

Harold took position with his army on top of a hill about 8 km (5 miles) from Hastings. When William and his army arrived on 14 October, they saw that they would have to fight uphill.

The battle raged all day. During the afternoon a rumour spread that William had been killed, and his troops began to

lose heart. William took off his helmet so that he could be seen, and rode up and down to show his men he was still alive. That put fresh heart into the invaders.

As evening approached, William's men made a rush at the Anglo-Saxon shield wall, and then pretended to retreat in order to draw their enemies away from their tightly held line. Harold's men broke ranks to pursue them, and were caught in William's trap. The Normans then rushed Harold's shield wall, and King Harold fell, with most of his Anglo-Saxon nobles.

William was crowned King in Westminster Abbey on Christmas Day 1066, becoming William I of England. He is more famously known by the name of William the Conqueror.

The Domesday Book
William wanted to know what his new kingdom was worth, who held what land, and how wealthy his subjects were. In 1086, he sent out agents to do a huge census of the whole population, and the results were recorded in the Domesday (Doomsday) Book.

The Bayeaux Tapestry
This embroidery is 82.3 m (270 ft) long and 0.51 m (20 in.) wide, and tells the story of the Battle of Hastings and events leading up to it from the Norman point of view. Bayeaux is in Normandy.

Westminster
Abbey, London

Olympic Games

In ancient times the Olympic Games were held in a place called Olympia, on the south-western Greek mainland. No one knows exactly when they were first held, but from 776 BC the Greeks started making a note of the date for the Games. The Olympic Games were held in honour of Zeus, the king of the gods.

At first only one race (the sprint) was run, and the Games lasted one day. Gradually more events were added, and by the end of the 5th century BC the Games lasted for five days. Only Greek male citizens were allowed to compete in the Games.

The festival

By the 1st century AD, Olympia had been transformed by the construction of magnificent stone temples and sports facilities. Two days before the start of the Olympic festival all the participants set out from Elis to walk 58 km (36 miles) to Olympia. This route was called the Sacred Way.

There were no awards for second or third place, but the winner received a wreath woven from a branch of the sacred olive tree in the Altis. This holy place was where the ancient Greeks believed the god Zeus lived in his great temple. The religious ending to the festival was the sacrifice to Zeus of 100 oxen.

Q&A?

Do you know why the Olympic flag has five rings?

The rings on the Olympic flag stand for the world's five continents, which are linked together by competing in the multi-national games.

Which swimmer holds the record for winning the most gold medals at one Olympic Games?

The American Mark Spitz holds the record. He won seven golds in swimming events at the 1972 Munich Games.

Banning the games

The Games gradually became more about pleasing the spectators than the gods. The final Olympic festival was held when the Christian Emperor of Rome, Theodosius I, banned the worship of non-Christian gods.

The Olympics were revived in June 1896 by Baron Pierre de Coubertin, who believed passionately that international sports competitions were a way to build friendship between nations.

The modern games

In 1896, nearly 250 men from different countries completed against one another for ten days and in 43 events. The modern Olympics are not religious and, since 1900, women have been allowed to take part.

The Paralympics

Since 1960 there has been a third kind of Olympics – for less able athletes. These Games are called the Paralympics, and they take place every four years, about the same time as the Summer Olympics. Paralympic events include all sorts of sports, from basketball to rhythmic gymnastics.

The marathon

The longest Olympic running race is the marathon. Athletes have to complete a course of about 42 km (26 miles). The event is named after a great Greek victory over Persian invaders in 490 BC. According to a later legend, a Greek messenger ran all the way from Marathon to Athens with the joyful news, then dropped dead.

Fascinating facts

At the 1988 Paralympic Games, held at Seoul in South Korea, Denmark's wheelchair athlete Connie Hansen won five events. She was first in the 400 m, 800 m, 1500 m, 5,000 m and wheelchair marathon races. At the next Paralympics in 1992, in Barcelona, Spain, she won the marathon again!

Since the Amsterdam Games in 1928, a special flame burns at all Olympic venues. Since 1936 this flame has been brought from Olympia in Greece, and is usually carried by torch-bearers.

Prehistory

Prehistory, or 'before history', is the period of human evolution before written records. Palaeontologists study fossils, tools and paintings to work out how people lived.

Prehistory is divided into three broad ages of prehistoric people: Stone Age, Bronze Age and Iron Age. These names are based on the technology used during the different periods. New artefacts (objects) are still being discovered, providing new information about what the world was like for early human beings.

The Stone Age

The Stone Age or 'Neolithic' period was 2 million years ago. Tools and weapons were made from stone, and people hunted animals, fished with simple weapons, gathered food such as berries from plants, and discovered fire.

Archaeologists have found cave paintings, which show that early people produced artwork, such as rock paintings called 'petroglyphs'. Early humans also used dyes to decorate their bodies, and there is evidence that some of them used copper ore to produce basic tools. Very hard rocks like flint were shaped to use as cutting tools or arrowheads. There was an increasing use of technology, and a gradual development of agriculture. Dogs were used for hunting, and lived with their masters.

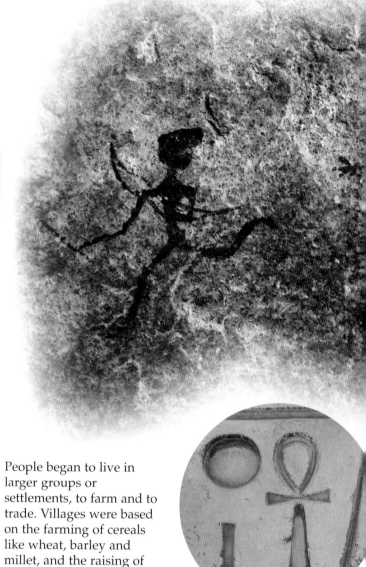

People began to live in larger groups or settlements, to farm and to trade. Villages were based on the farming of cereals like wheat, barley and millet, and the raising of cattle, sheep, goats and pigs.

The Bronze Age

The Bronze Age in Britain is considered to have been from around 2100 BC to 700 BC. Metalworking began during this period, and bronze tools were increasingly common and useful. There was skilled and detailed workmanship, producing many beautiful objects such as carved drinking horns and decorated pottery. There were also some early forms of writing, such as Egyptian hieroglyphs and Mayan symbols.

The first use of iron occurred in Ancient Egypt around 4000 BC. Spear tips and beads were fashioned from iron found in meteorites.

Skara Brae on the island of Orkney, off the coast of Scotland, is a Neolithic village discovered by archaeologists. Here archaeologists found stone beds and shelves, and even an indoor toilet connected to a nearby stream.

fascinating
Facts

A cave painting

The search for more raw materials led to exploration and colonisation of new territories. Trade routes enabled travellers to reach other countries. Cities were formed and countries emerged, but traders became rivals and competition for raw materials led to wars. Communities built boats, developed farming techniques and invented new technology, for example the ox-drawn plough.

The Iron Age

The Iron Age in Britain is considered to have been from around 5th century BC until the Roman conquest in England and until the 5th century AD in other parts of Britain. Iron tools and weapons were made in this period, which ended with the development of written history. Different parts of the world advanced at different speeds. The Greek and Roman Empires and their great cultures were very advanced, but in Northern Europe the Iron Age lasted until the early Middle Ages.

Iron was hard, had a high melting point, and there was a lot of iron ore available. So having once been rare and costly, iron was now a cheap and useful material, and became used for many different tasks.

Iron allowed warfare to become more sophisticated. There was fighting on horseback and in horse-drawn chariots, and swords and arrows were produced from iron.

Coins were manufactured in bronze, making trade easier. Iron-made tools were stronger and better, and people's lives improved because of higher agricultural productivity. Iron-tipped ploughs were more efficient than wooden ones, and iron axes cut down trees quickly – clearing land for farming, and providing wood for building.

Q&A?

What was the most important invention of the Bronze age?

The wheel. This allowed people to make carts and transport goods.

How is bronze made?

Bronze is a mixture of copper, tin and other metals.

The Romans

Around 2,000 years ago, the Roman Empire dominated Europe. It ruled lands around the Mediterranean from France to Turkey to North Africa. It came to an end in 476 AD.

The city of Rome

Rome was the capital city of the Roman Empire, and today is the capital city of Italy. It was famous for being built on seven hills. At first, Rome was ruled by kings, but the last king, Tarquin the Proud, was overthrown in 510 BC and Rome became a Republic. A republic is a form of government that is not ruled by a monarch (king or queen). The Republic was ruled for 400 years by a council called the Senate.

The Roman army

Over time, the generals of the Roman army became very powerful, and started to control government. However, they tended to argue among themselves, and eventually just one man took over – Rome had an Emperor.

The Romans were able to keep and expand their Empire thanks to their army. They had the first professional army of paid soldiers in the

world. Soldiers were brought into the army from all parts of the Empire, and sent to fight far away from their homes. The army was organised as follows:

- The army was divided into legions of 5,000 men. There were about 30 legions.
  - Each legion was divided into ten cohorts.
  - Each cohort was divided into six centuries. A century contained 80 men and was commanded by an officer called a Centurion.
  - Each century was divided into ten groups of eight men who lived, travelled and fought together.

What did a Roman soldier wear?

The Roman soldiers were very well-equipped. Ordinary soldiers wore leather sandals, wool tunics and leather breeches. They had armour made from overlapping iron bands. They carried a curved shield (called a scutum) and had a bronze helmet. Each man carried a sword (called a gladius), two javelins and a dagger.

Roman towns

The Romans built towns in all the lands they conquered. They were all built to the same plan. Streets were arranged in a criss-cross pattern. Two main streets divided the town, with smaller streets built off them at right angles.

Q&A?

What did Roman women wear?

Roman women wore a garment called a stola, a long dress of fine woollen cloth that came to their ankles. They often wore their hair curled and up on top of their heads, and were fond of jewellery.

What did the Roman men wear?

Roman men wore knee-length tunics, belted at the waist, and sandals. For important occasions they would wear a toga, a drape of fine wool cloth that went around and over the body, covering the right shoulder.

fascinating facts

The first Roman Emperor was called Augustus. He came to power in 27 BC.

Walls were built round the town for protection, and people could only enter or leave by gates.

Rich people lived in well-built town houses, but poor people lived in cheap blocks of apartments, some up to four storeys high. Rich houses had central heating, plumbing, gardens and lovely decorations like mosaic floors.

The Roman town

You could find the following buildings in any Roman town:

Forum – Important buildings like offices and law courts were built around this 'town square', and a market was often held here.

Baths – the Romans built large public bathhouses called thermae. People went there to get clean but also to relax and meet friends. As well as bathing, they could exercise there in the gymnasium.

Amphitheatre – where public entertainments like gladiator contests and chariot races were held. There is a picture of one at the bottom of this page.

Basilica – this was something like the town hall, where government took place.

Roman engineering

Central heating – public baths and the houses of rich people had central heating! Floors were built on top of a series of 'tunnels' called a hypocaust – hot air from a furnace travelled through these tunnels, heating the floors and rooms above.

Plumbing – Roman houses had the best drains in the ancient world. Underground drains took away waste water and sewage, and were flushed through with water from the baths.

Aqueducts – Roman towns had piped water. If water had to be brought from a long way away, they would build huge aqueducts (a kind of bridge that carried water on the top of it) across valleys.

Roads – long, straight 'Roman roads' were built wherever the Romans went, and many can still be seen today.

The Vikings

The Vikings lived in Scandinavia (Denmark, Norway and Sweden) around 750-1100 AD. Villages all round the coasts of Europe lived in terror of their raids, but they also travelled in peace. Vikings were traders, selling weapons, timber, jewels, pottery, spices and honey in their impressive ships.

What has been written about the Vikings?

Much of what we know about the Vikings comes from their sagas (stories), which were written in Iceland in the 13th and 14th centuries. The Vikings themselves did not write things down, though they did carve 'picture words' called runes into wood and stone.

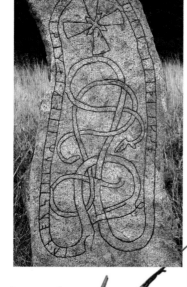

Written stories we have about the Vikings were provided by English and French monks, whose settlements were often attacked by the Vikings. These accounts describe Vikings as terrifying savages.

Viking ships

The Vikings built wonderful ships, called longships. They had a high prow (front) and stern (back) to help them glide through rough waters. The prow was often decorated with a fearsome carved dragon's head.

The ships were built of wood. Tar from pine trees was used to waterproof them. They had square sails, and could be rowed by oarsmen if there was no wind. A large oar at the back of the ship was used for steering.

Longships could sail up shallow rivers, and could be run right up onto the beach at the start of a raid so that the Vikings could leap straight out, ready to fight.

Viking weapons and armour

Our knowledge about Viking weapons and armour is based on a relatively few archaeological finds, pictures and to some extent, on the sagas.

All free Norse men were required to own weapons and were allowed to carry them at all times. The weapons indicated how rich a man was. A wealthy Viking would have a helmet, shield, chainmail shirt and animal-skin coat. Someone who was less wealthy would only be able to afford a simple weapon and, perhaps, a shield.

What was everyday life like for a Viking?

The Vikings weren't just warriors and explorers – they were also settlers and farmers. Most of them lived on farms. Their chiefs lived in huge longhouses with wood or stone walls and straw-covered roofs. Families and servants all shared one big room. A hole in the roof was the only way to let smoke escape, and the longhouses would have been very dark as they had no windows.

In the cold of winter, even farm animals would be kept inside the longhouse.

The Vikings' clothes were made from wool, linen and leather. They loved bright colours, and made red and green dyes from berries, and yellow and green dyes from vegetables.

They loved jewellery and dressed up their outfits with rings, arm rings, brooches, fancy buckles and necklaces.

How did the Vikings find their way across the seas?

They had to make their way using the position of the sun and stars and the direction of the wind, and by keeping an eye out for familiar landmarks on the shore.

What sort of weapons did the Vikings have?

Vikings treasured their weapons. In the sagas, Viking warriors give their heavy swords, spears and battle-axes special names, like 'Leg Biter' and 'War flame'.

Were the Vikings the first Europeans to discover America?

Their sagas (stories) tell us that they were! They tell the story of the hero Leif Ericsson, who discovered a new and rich land by sailing far to the West from his home in Greenland. He called it Vinland.

What's the story?

In 986 AD, a Viking trader named Bjarni Herjollfsson set sail from Iceland to Greenland. He was blown off course, and after many days sighted unfamiliar land, covered in forest, to the West. This could not be Greenland, which was always covered with ice. When he finally got home to Greenland, Bjarni told stories about the strange land he had seen.

Leif was determined to find this new land, and he set off westward with 35 men. By winter they had arrived, and become the first Europeans to set foot on the continent of North America.

What's the evidence?

In the 1960s, archaeologists excavated a typical Viking settlement camp at the tip of Newfoundland, in Canada. We cannot say for certain that this is the place found by Leif, but it certainly proves that the Vikings were on American soil more than 1000 years ago.

'Viking' comes from the Old Norse word vika, which means 'to go off'. They are also called the Norse, or Norsemen.

People in Iceland today can still read the Viking sagas, because the Icelandic language has stayed the same for hundreds of years.

Many people believe they were also the first Europeans to discover America – 500 years before Columbus ever got there!

Silver jewellery was used in place of money. A Viking buying a pig from his neighbour would take off his silver arm ring, and break off a piece to pay for the pig.

Fascinating Facts

Wonders of the World

The Seven Wonders of the World are famous structures built many years ago. The list was made in the second century BC, and only includes the Mediterranean part of the world. Six out of the seven ancient wonders have been destroyed, but fragments remain, and there are descriptions of them in old books.

The Pyramids at Giza

This is the only one that still exists. There are three pyramids near Cairo in Egypt, the largest of which is 150 m (450 ft) high, containing 2.3 million stone blocks each weighing about 2,268 kg (2.5 tons). They were built by the Egyptian pharaoh Khufu, and finished in 2680 BC. The Great Pyramid was built as Khufu's tomb. The other two large pyramids are the Pyramid of Khafre and the Pyramid of Menkaure.

The Hanging Gardens of Babylon

We don't know if these really existed. They were supposedly built in present-day Iraq by King Nebuchadnezzer in 600 BC to please his queen, and were thought to have been terraced gardens on top of a building, between 25 and 100 m (75 and 300 ft) high. Greek historians wrote about the gardens, but otherwise there is little evidence for their existence. Archaeologists have found ruined foundations of a large palace that could have been the building the gardens were built upon.

The Statue of Zeus at Olympia

This was 13.3 m (40 ft) high and was made from ivory and gold by a famous Greek sculptor called Phidias in about 435 BC. It was lost (probably in a fire) but was pictured on old Greek coins. The statue is of the Greek god Zeus.

The Temple of Artemis at Ephesus

This was built in 350 BC, with columns 20 m (60 ft) high, for the goddess Artemis (also known as Diana, the goddess of the moon). It took 120 years to build, and was a large marble temple with much fine artwork and sculpture inside. The beauty of the temple attracted many tourists and worshippers. It was destroyed by fire when the Goths invaded in AD 262. Only a single column remains from the original temple.

The Mausoleum at Halicarnassus

This was a huge white marble tomb built at Halicarnassus in about 355 BC by Queen Artemisia. It was a shrine in memory of her husband, and also held his remains. It was designed by Greek architects and was 45 m (135 ft) high